Low
Voice
Solos

Low
Voice
Solos

Compiled and Edited by
Bryce Inman

WORD MUSIC

Printed by Davis Brothers Publishing Co., Inc., Waco, TX

TOPICAL INDEX

(CONT.)

TOPICAL INDEX
(CONT.)

CONTENTS

I Pledge Allegiance to the Lamb

Words and Music by
RAY BOLTZ

With conviction ♩ = 76

I___ pledge al - le - giance to the___ Lamb, with___ all my strength, with all I___ am. I will seek to hon - or His com - mands. I___ pledge al - le - giance___ to___ the___ Lamb.

1. I have

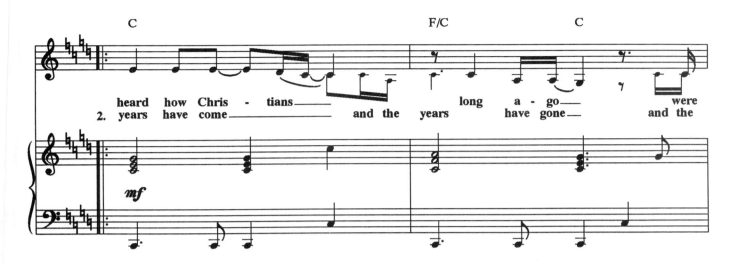

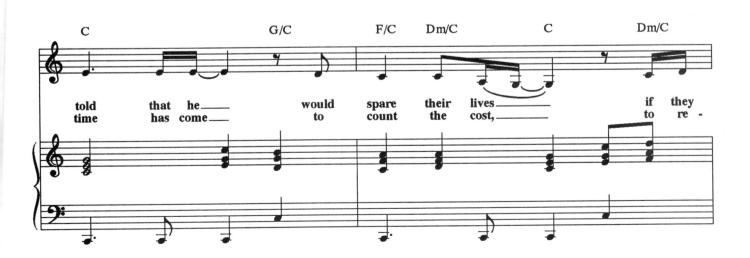

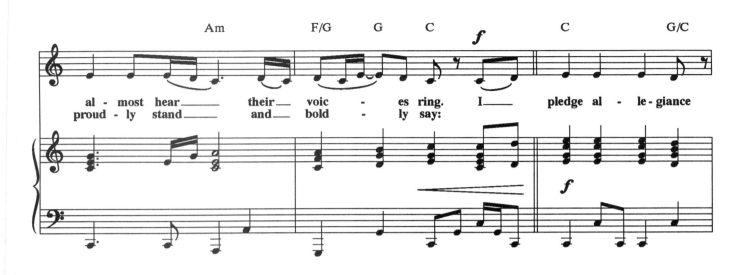

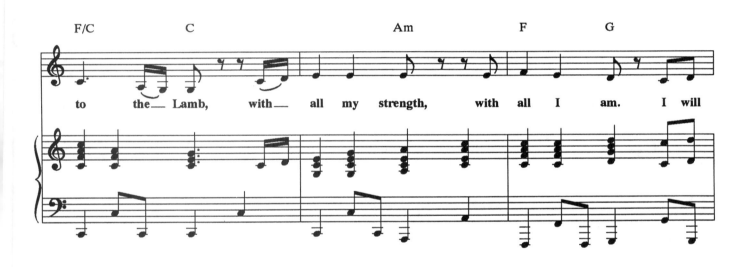

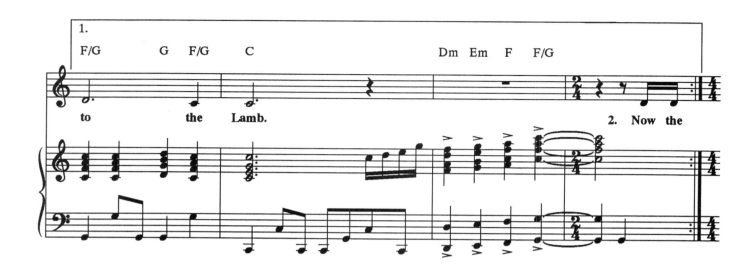

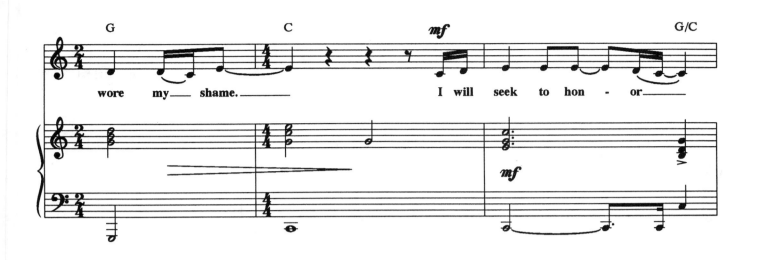

Carry On
with
Holy Lord

Worshipfully

"Holy Lord" - Words and Music by Sandi Patty

Lord, You are the life in me, ___ Your love is all I need. For - ev - er,

ho - ly Lord, You are the life in me,___ Your love is

all I need. You are my God and King. You are for - ev - er ho - ly.___

With strength ♩ = 72
"Carry On" - Words: Bob Farrell; Music: Michael W. Smith

Fno3   Fno3/E   Fno3/D   Fno3/C

Fno3   Fno3/E   Fno3/D   Fno3/C

Bb2(no3)

C Bb2/D F2 F2/E
car - ry on. O, God of awe - some might,
F/D F/C Bb2 Gm/Bb C Am/C
You draw me to Your light, car - ry on, car - ry on,
2nd time to
Dm Bb/D F/C Csus C Bb2
car - ry on. My life is in Your hands, car - ry on.
C/Bb Bb2
mp
Car - ry on.

My life is in Your hands,

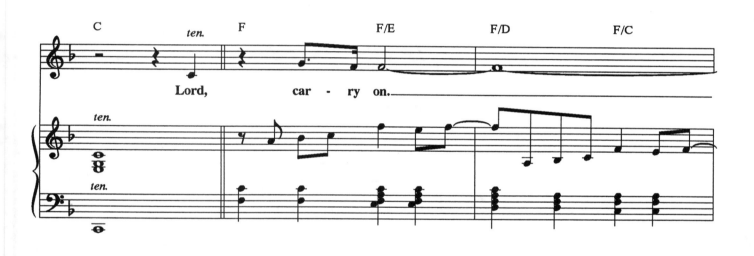

Lord, car - ry on.

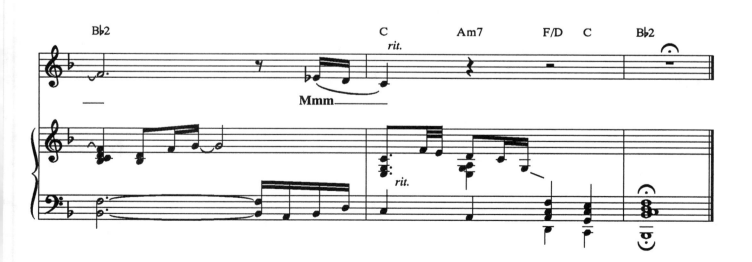

Mmm

With All My Heart

Words and Music by
BABBIE MASON

Freely, with emotion ♩ = 58

1. In this qu-iet place with You,— I bow be-fore Your throne. I bare the deep-est part of me to

You and You a-lone. I keep no se-crets, for there is no thought You have not known.— I

bring my best, and all the rest, to You and— lay them down.

Written in Red

Words and Music by
GORDON JENSEN

Quietly ♩ =80

In let-ters_____ of crim-son God wrote His love on a

hill - side so long, long a - go. For you and for

He's Been Faithful

Words and Music by
CAROL CYMBALA

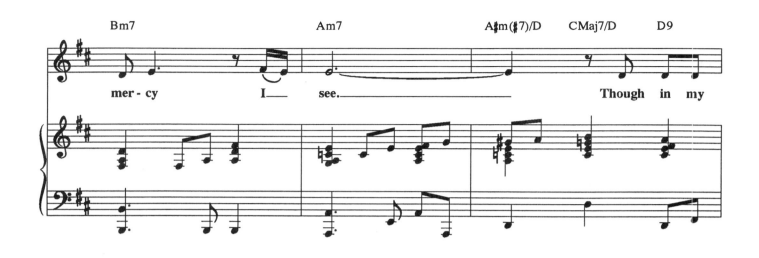

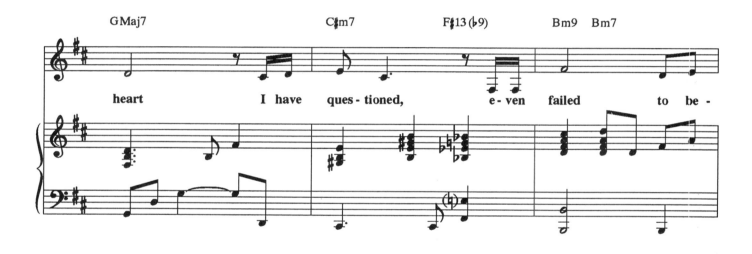

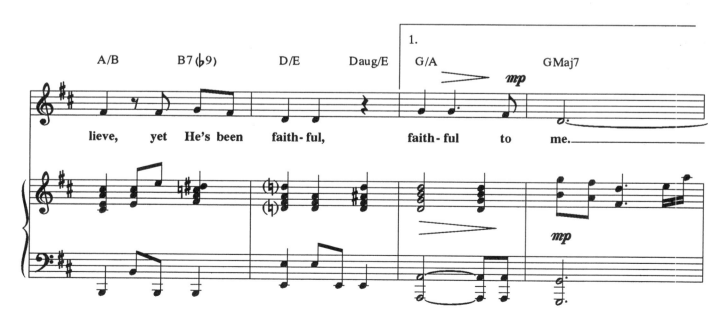

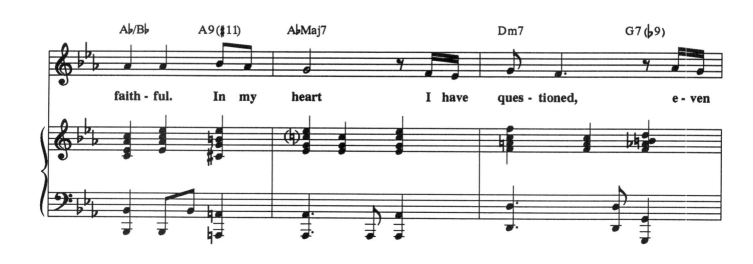

The Sea of Forgetfulness

Words and Music by
BABBIE MASON
and **KENNY MANN**

I Will Be Here for You

Words and Music by
MICHAEL W. SMITH
and DIANE WARREN

Steady four ♩ = 69

1. When you feel the sun - light fade in - to the cold night,
2. In this world of strang - ers, of cold and friend - ly fac - es

(Don't know where to turn, I don't know where to turn) and
(Some - one you can trust, oh, there's some - one you can trust). and

all the dreams— you're— dream - ing   seem to lose— their mean - ing,—
I will be— your— shel - ter,   I'll give you my shoul - der—

(Let me in— your world,— ba - by, let me in— your world)—
(Reach out for— my love,— reach out for— my love).—

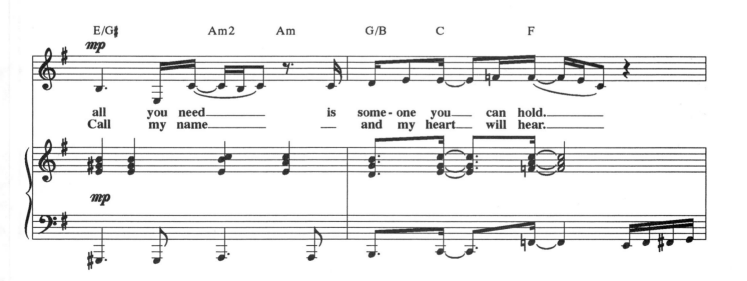

all you need— is some - one you— can hold.—
Call my name— and my heart— will hear.—

For the Cause of Christ

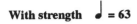

Words and Music by
BABBIE MASON

With strength ♩ = 63

1. Man-y trust in kings and queens___ whose names we could re-call;___

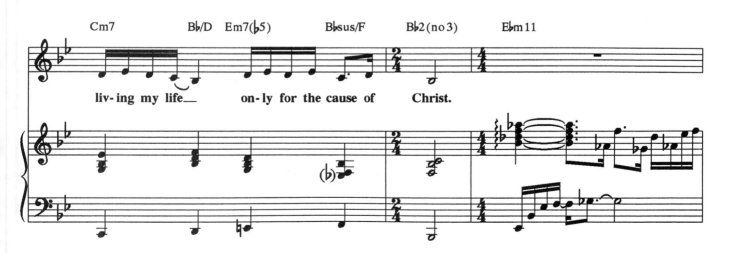

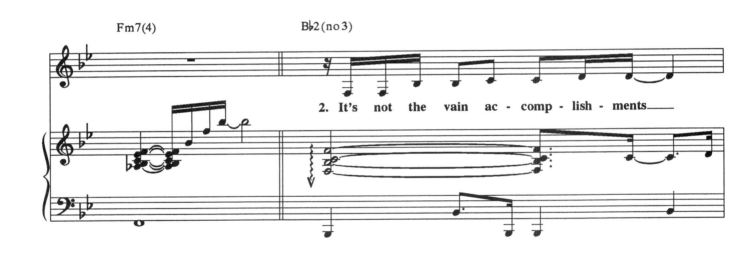

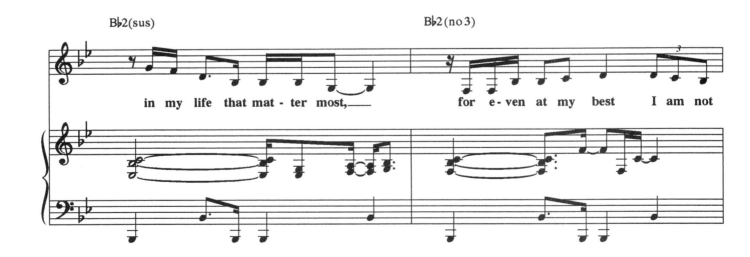

D. S. al Coda 𝄋

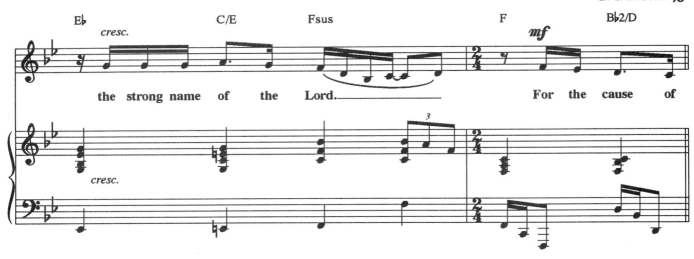

the strong name of the Lord._____ For the cause of

● CODA

liv - ing my___ life on - ly for the cross of Christ. I must for -

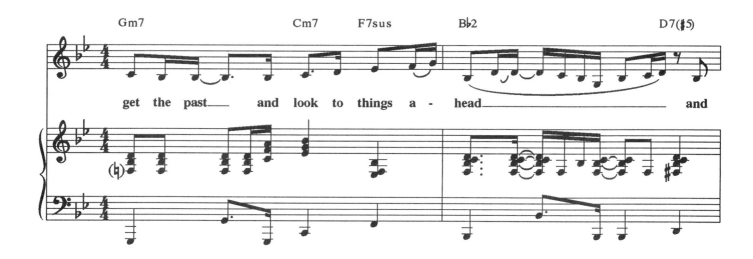

get the past___ and look to things a - head_____ and

Home Free

Words and Music by
WAYNE WATSON

1. I'm try - ing

There Is Prayer

Words and Music by
BRUCE CARROLL
and JOHN G. ELLIOTT

Serve the Lord

Words and Music by
CARMAN

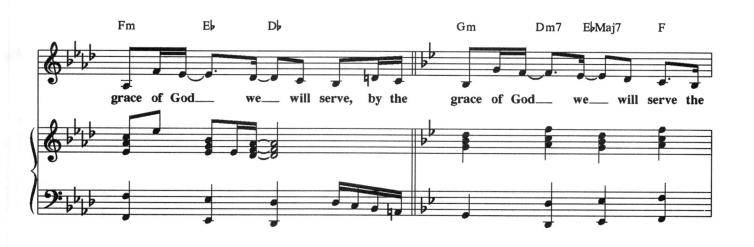

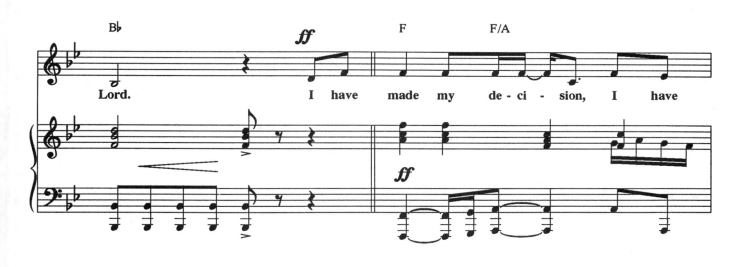

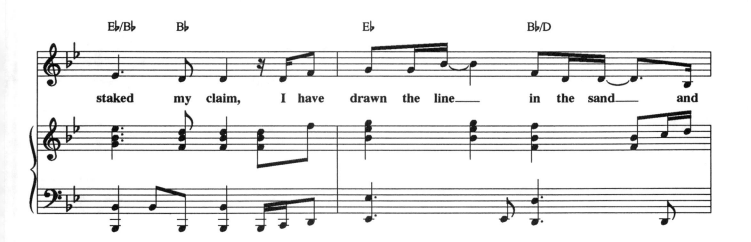

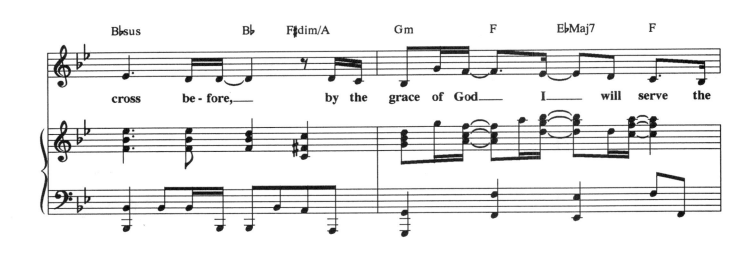

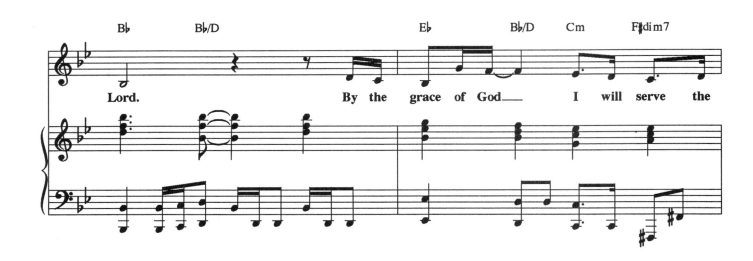

Lord. By the grace of God___ I will serve___ the

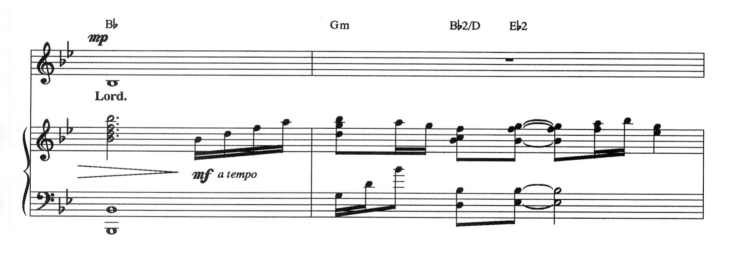

Lord.

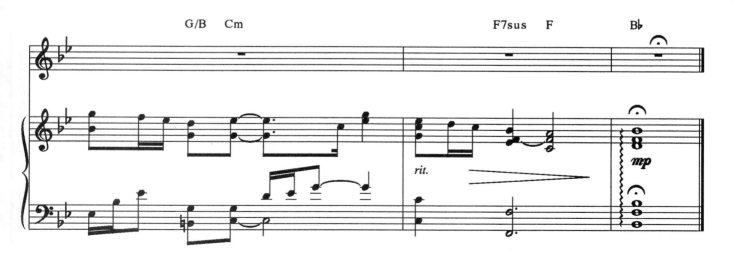

All Across the Sky

Words and Music by
JON MOHR
and **MICHAEL W. SMITH**

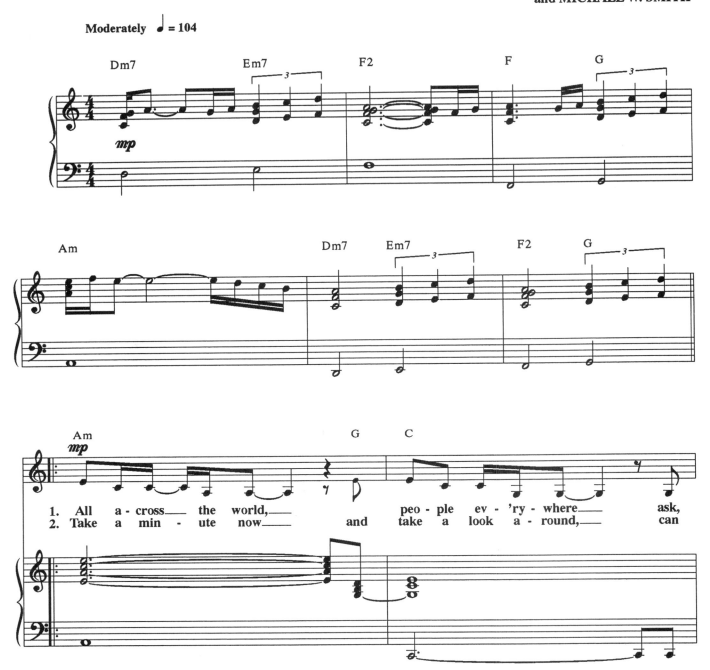

Rise Up, O Men of God

Words and Music by
WILLIAM MERRILL, WILLIAM WALTER
BILL BATSTONE and BUDDY OWENS

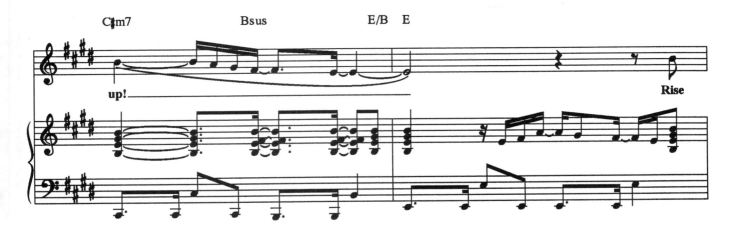

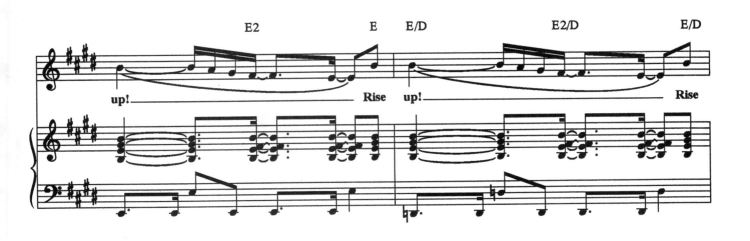

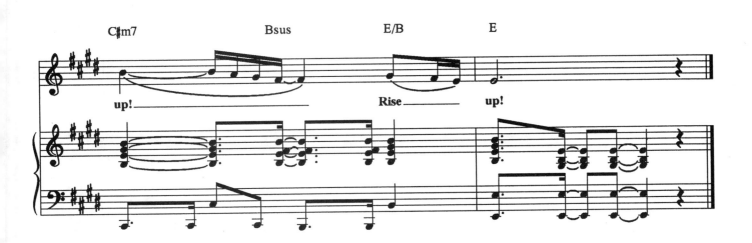

Come Worship the Lord

Words and Music by
TWILA PARIS

With a two feel ♩ = 160

Come, wor-ship the Lord God Al-might-y for

Heaven Is Counting on You

Words and Music by
RAY BOLTZ
and STEVE MILLIKAN

With energy ♩ = 100

God Will Make a Way

Words and Music by
DON MOEN

Miracle of Mercy

Words and Music by
STEVEN CURTIS CHAPMAN

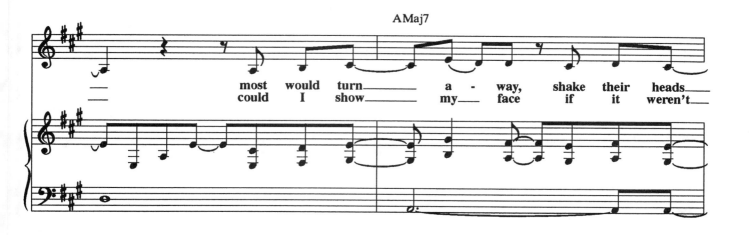

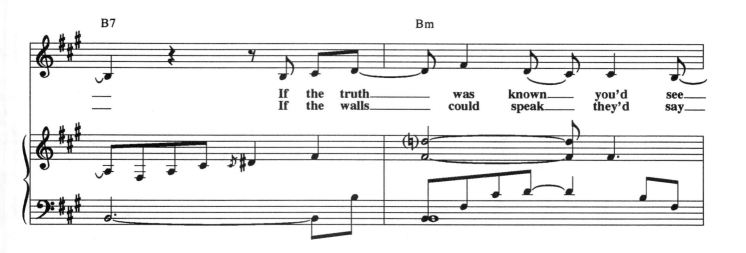

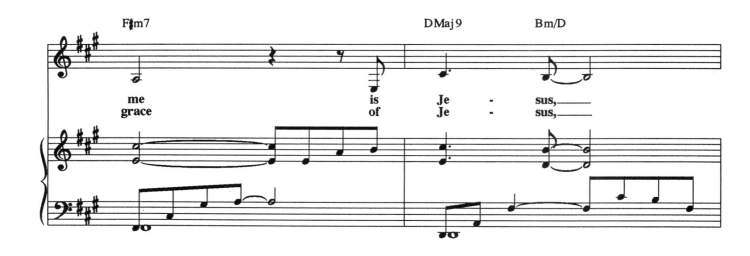

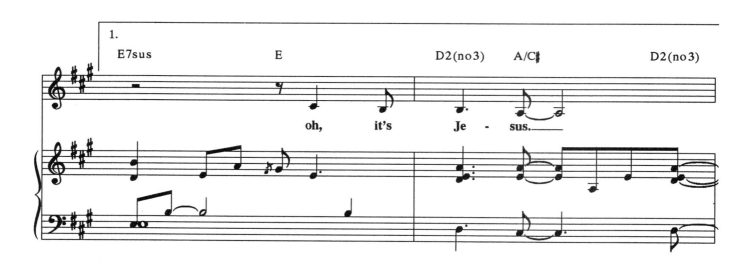

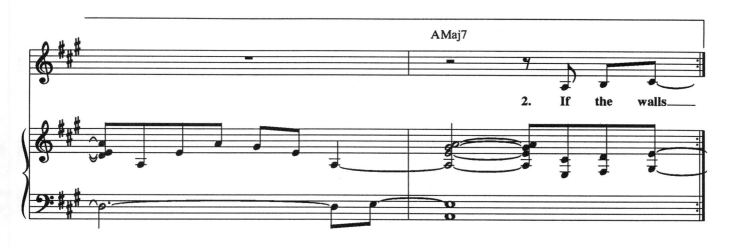

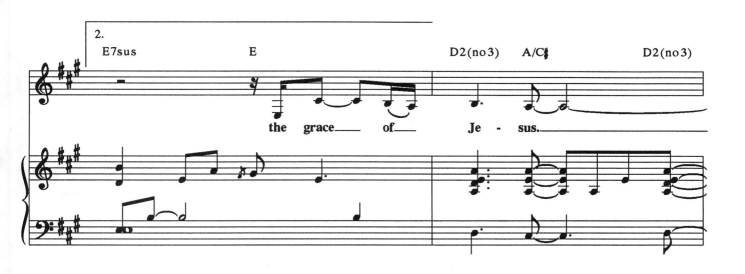

Jesus, the Sweetest Name of All

Words and Music by
BABBIE MASON and
DONNA DOUGLAS

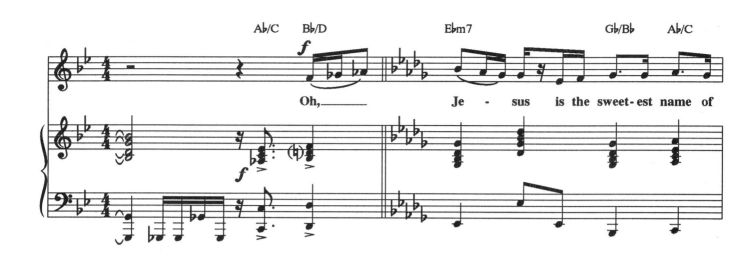

Oh,_____ Je - sus is the sweet - est name of

all._____ Who can con - quer the grave, who is a - ble to save__ but

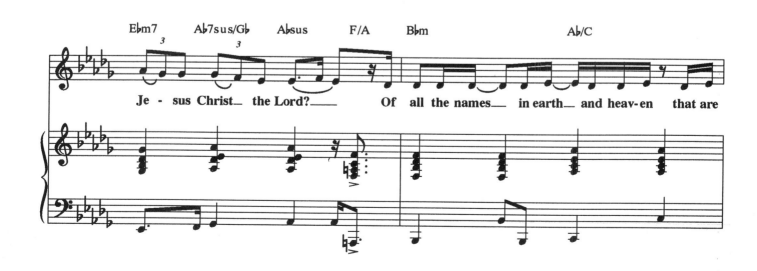

Je - sus Christ__ the Lord?__ Of all the names__ in earth__ and heav - en that are

beau - ti - ful___ to call, oh, Je - sus is the sweet - est

name_____ of all._____

How Beautiful

Words and Music by
TWILA PARIS

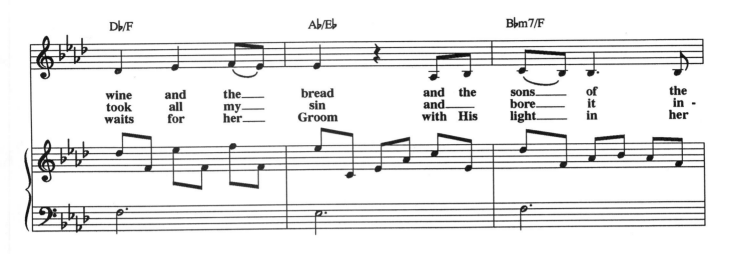

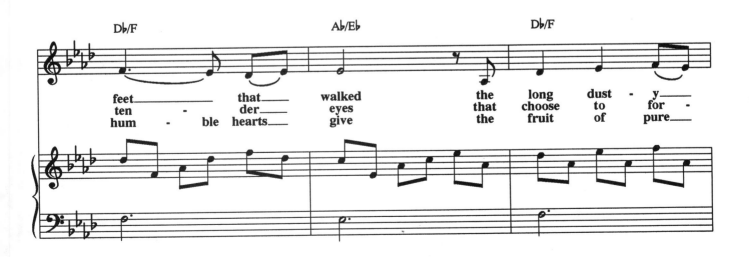

D. S. al Coda
rit.
price.
3. How
rit.
CODA
E♭/G
Fsus
cresc.
F/A
Bod - y of Christ.
Fsus/E♭
F/E♭ F/D F/C
B♭/D
How beau - ti -
B♭2/D
E♭
B♭/D
E♭
ful the feet that bring the sound of good

I'll Give You Peace

Words and Music by
DAWN THOMAS
and TOM YARBROUGH

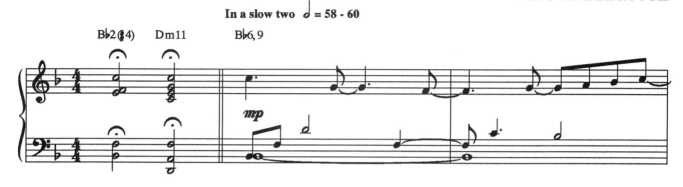

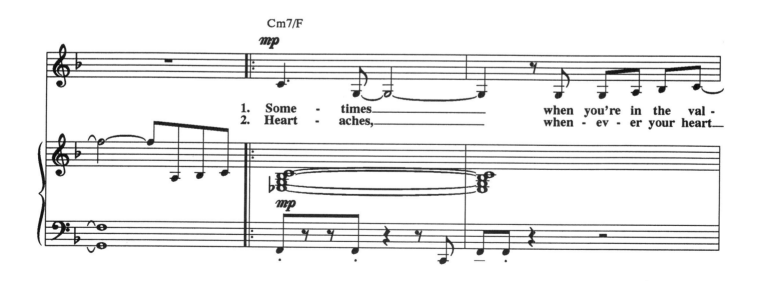

1. Some - times_____ when you're in the val -
2. Heart - aches,_____ when - ev - er your heart_

Dm11

I'll give you peace___ when the wind___

C/E   F2

___ starts blow - in'.

Dm11

I'll give you peace___ when the wind___

C/E   F2   *rit.*

___ starts blow - in'.___

rit.

Once and For All

Words and Music by
REGIE HAMM
and JOEL LINDSEY

To Be Like Jesus

Words and Music by
DICK and MELODIE TUNNEY

Slowly and freely

1. A lit - tle

girl is cry - ing_____ for af - fec - tion, a lit - tle

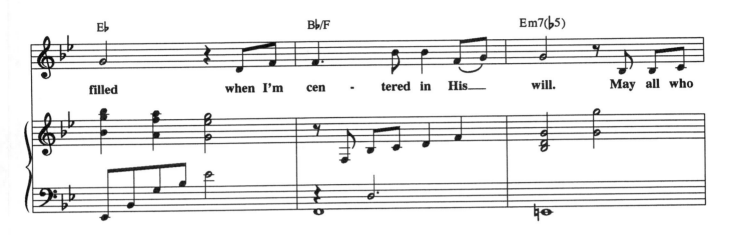

filled when I'm cen - tered in His___ will. May all who

see my heart find___ Him___ in me.

I Bowed on My Knees and Cried Holy

Composer Unknown
Arr. by Lari Goss

He Is Here

Words and Music by
KIRK TALLEY
Arr. by Don Wyrtzen

180

I know that there are an-gels hov-'ring all a-round us,_____ for the
I tast-ed all the things that sin could think to of-fer__ me, but to-

1.
pres-ence of the Lord___ is in this place. He is
day I feast on

2.
man-na from___ a-bove. He is

f With more intensity

here! Hal-le-lu-jah! He is here! A-men! He is

cresc.

here, ho - ly, ho - ly, I will bless His name a -

gain! He is here, lis - ten close - ly, hear Him call - ing out___ your

name; He is here, you can touch Him, you will nev - er be___ the

decresc.

decresc.

same! He is here, you can touch Him, you will

nev - er be___ the same. Nev - er be the

same, nev - er be the same.___

To the Cross

JULIE ADAMS

BABBIE MASON

With reverence

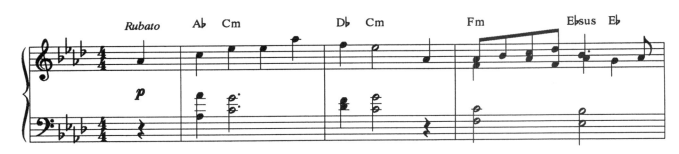

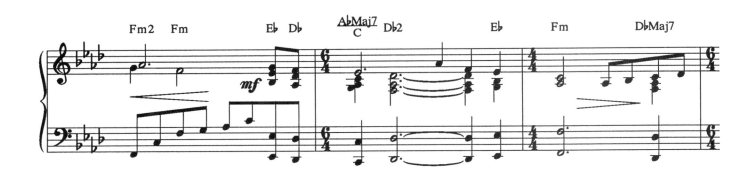

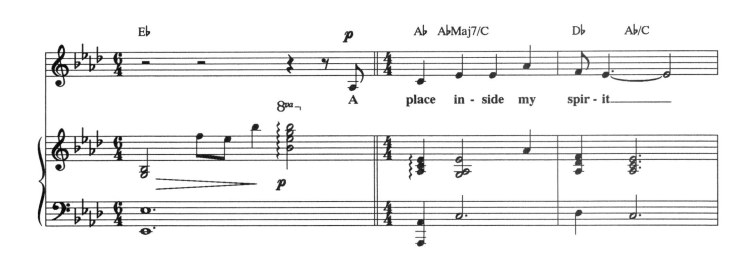

A place in - side my spir - it

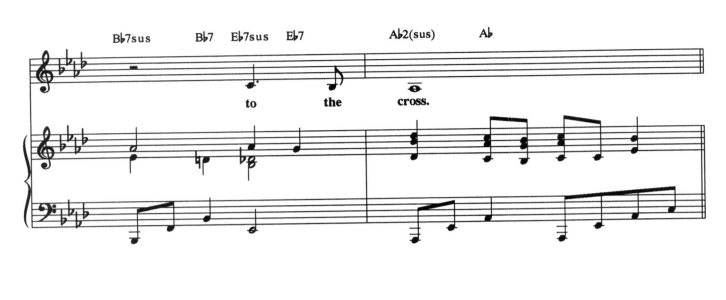

to the cross.

And there I lay them down

for the Sav - ior's love.   Be -

ter - mine this cross to be my friend. And

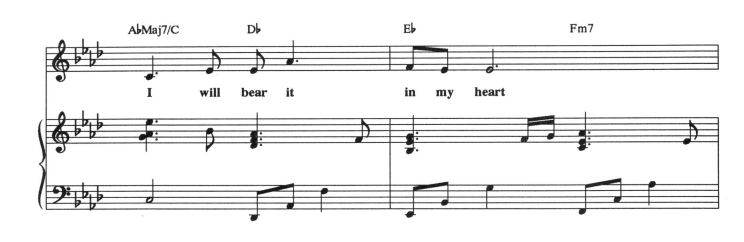

I will bear it in my heart

un - til my pride is dead. Part of me will

tell it "no,"_____ but Christ was there be -

fore me. So, I'll fol - low faith - ful - ly and go

to the cross. I'll

192

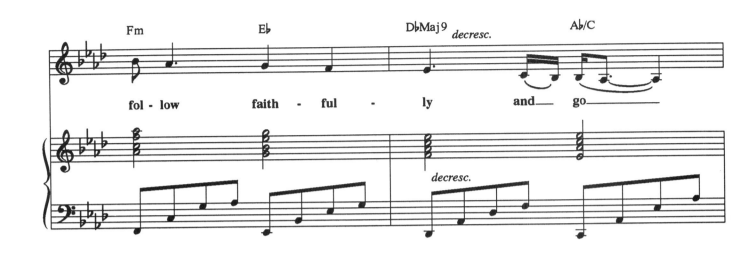

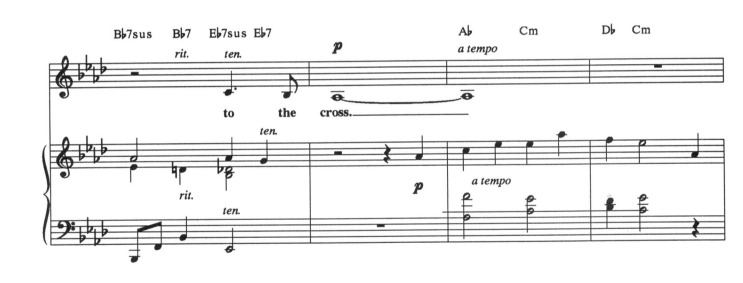

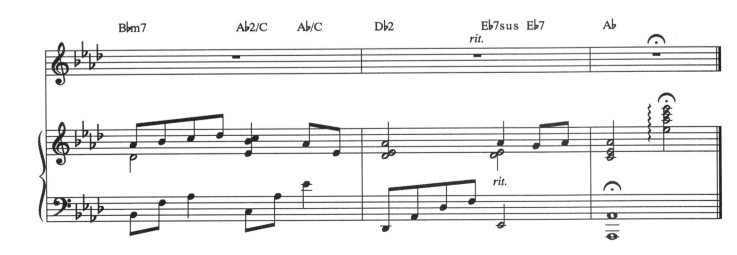

Lift Him Up

Words and Music by
BILLY FUNK

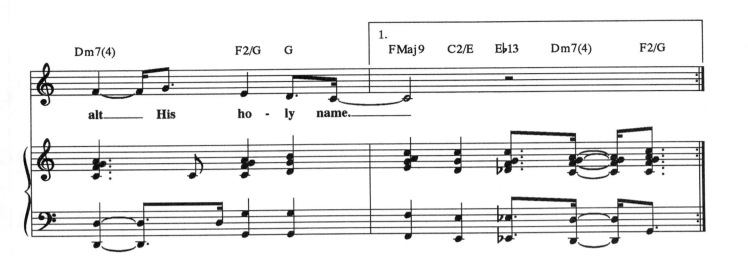

A Beautiful Place

Words and Music by
WAYNE WATSON

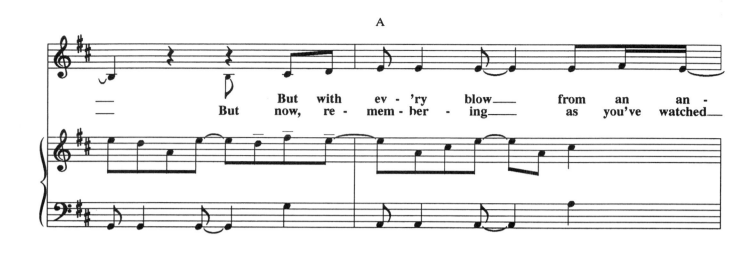

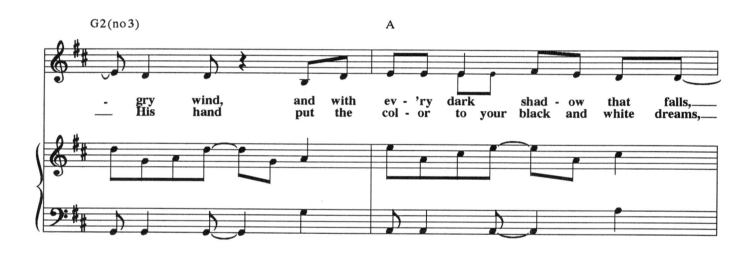

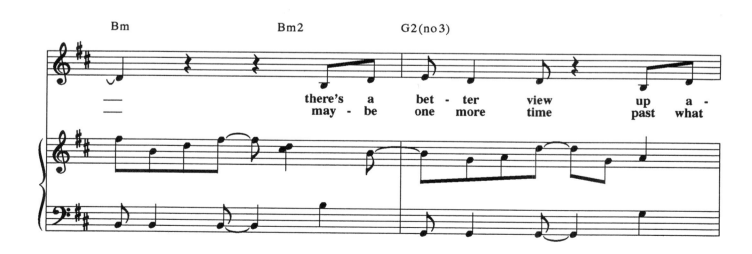

Still Listening

STEVEN CURTIS CHAPMAN
and GEOFF MOORE

STEVEN CURTIS CHAPMAN

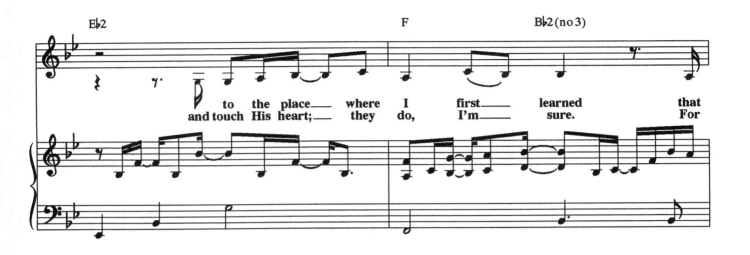

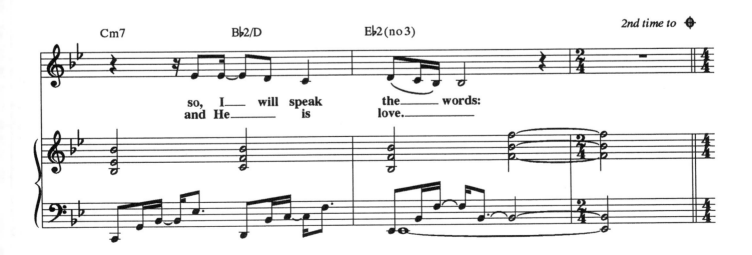

God Is Able

Rhythmically, with enthusiasm ♩=92

Words and Music by
HARLAN ROGERS

God is a - ble. God is a - ble.

224

Revive Us, Oh Lord

Words and Music by
CARMAN
and STEVE CAMP

Answer the Call

Words and Music by
JOHN MOHR
and PHIL NAISH

234

The River

Words and Music by
CARMAN

mat - ter who___ you are,___ it does-n't mat - ter where___ you've been;___ it does-n't
yond how far___ you've gone,___ He looks be - yond when you___ were hurt;___ He looks be-

(spoken: There is healing in Jesus' name!)

My Place Is with You

Words and Music by
MICHAEL PURYEAR
and **GEOFFREY THURMAN**

Innocent Eyes

Words and Music by
DAVID MARTIN
and WAYNE KIRKPATRICK

I of - fer you this___ prayer:___
I'd bear it all for___ you?___ May your

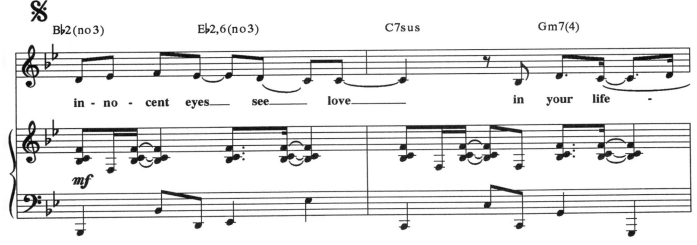

in - no - cent eyes___ see___ love___ in your life -

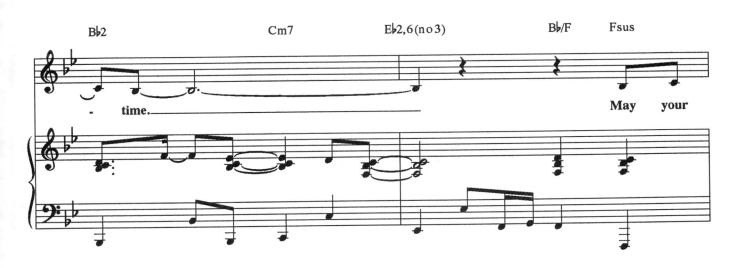

- time.___ May your

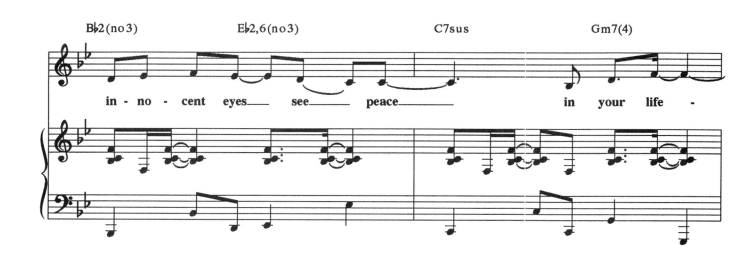

in - no - cent eyes___ see___ peace___ in your life -

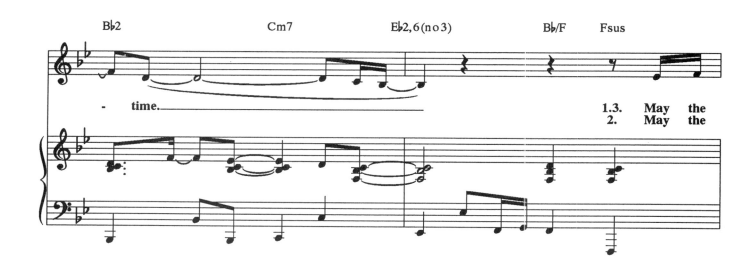

- time._____

1.3. May the
2. May the

wars all___ stop___ down and hun - ger___ fade,___
li - on___ lay___ down with the___ lamb,___

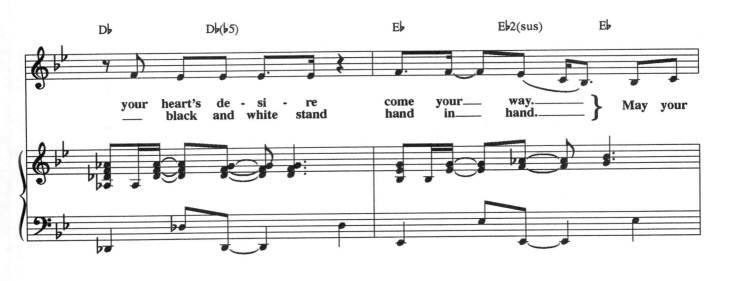

So much I would give to you; a life that's long and a

heart that's true. And may you love

some - one as much as I love you.

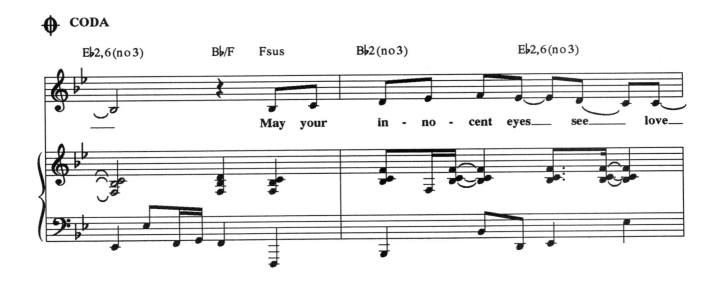

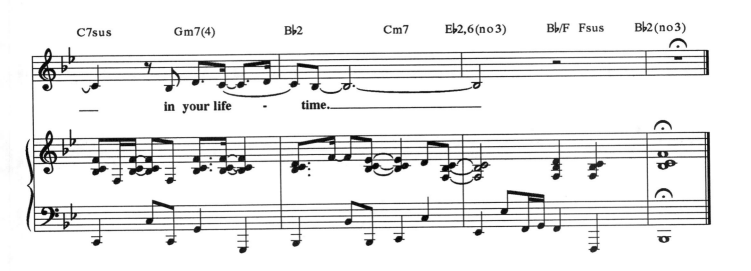

When I Heal

Words and Music by
CINDY MORGAN

With comfort ♩ = 108

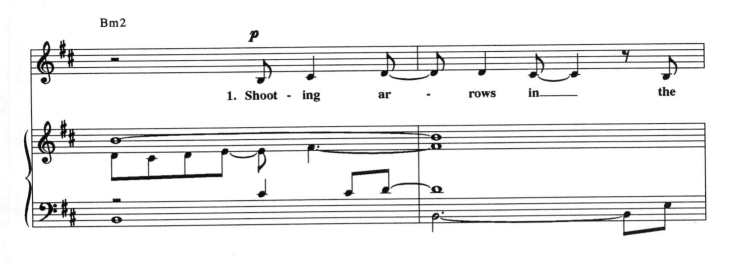

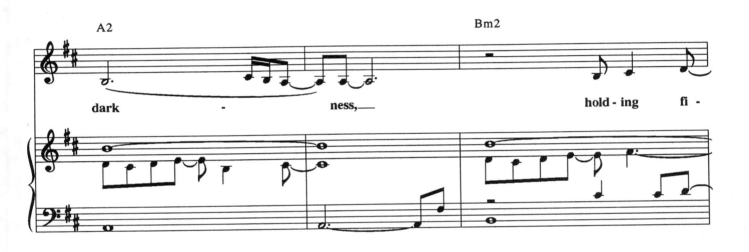

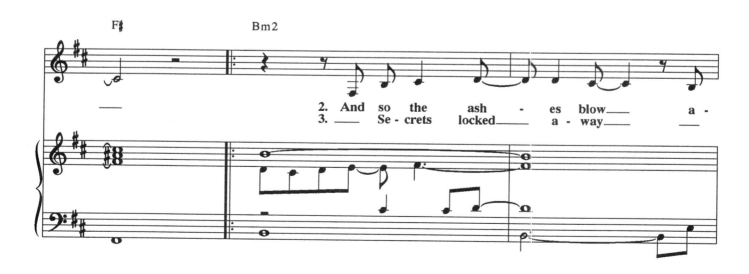

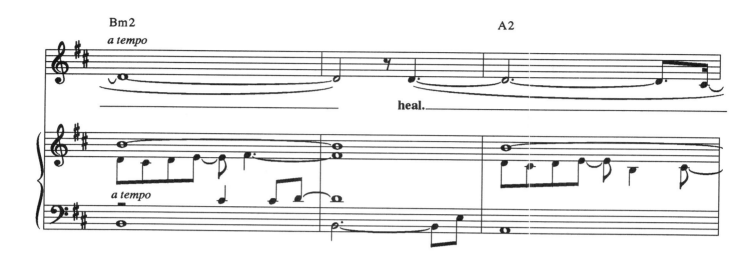

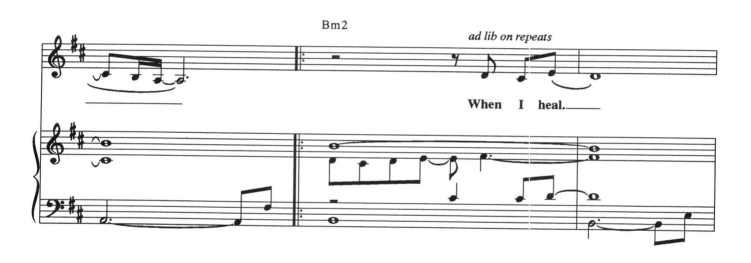

God Is in Control

Words and Music by
TWILA PARIS

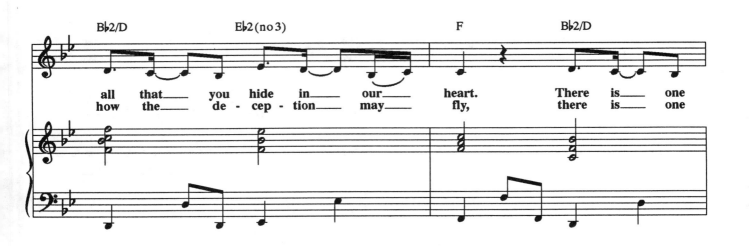

all that___ you hide in___ our___ heart. There is___ one
how the___ de - cep - tion___ may___ fly, there is___ one

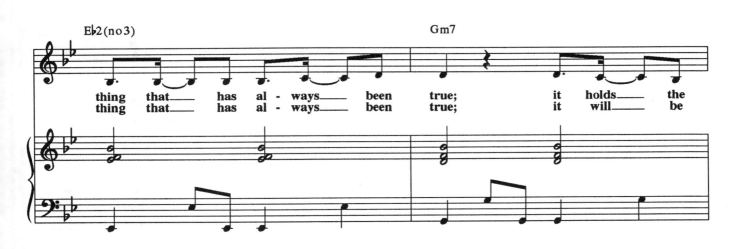

thing that___ has al - ways___ been true; it holds___ the
thing that___ has al - ways___ been true; it will___ be

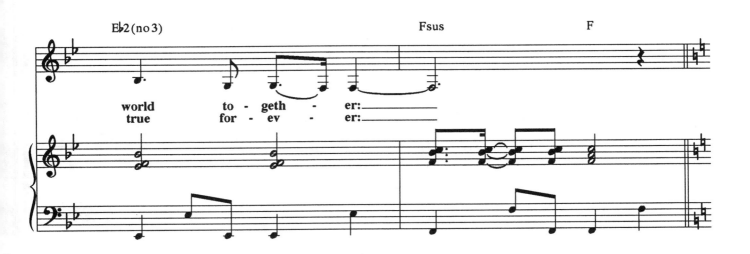

world to - geth - er:
true for - ev - er:

Kings Shall Bow

Words and Music by
GARY DRISKELL
and MARTY HENNIS

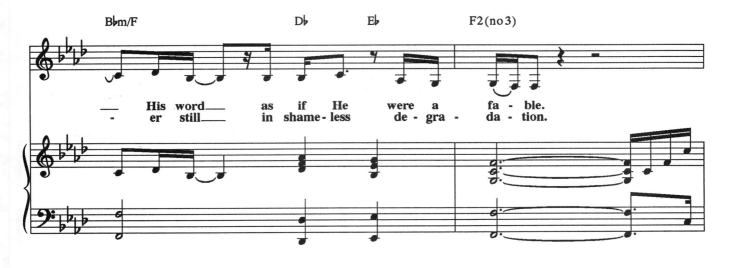

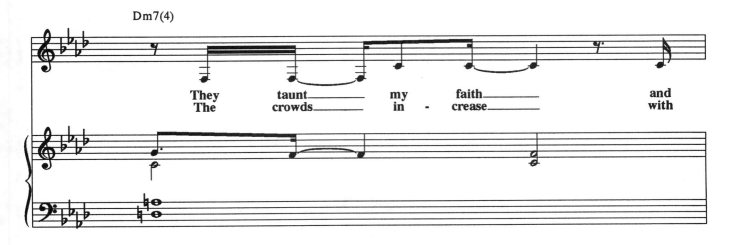

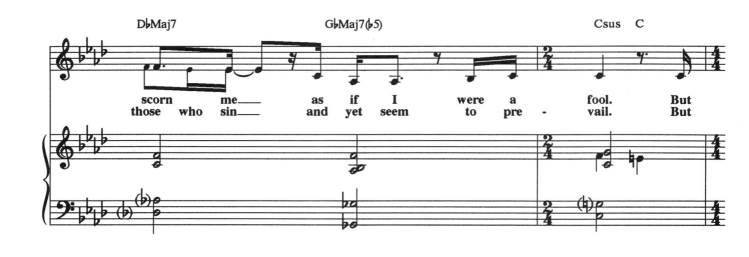

scorn me____ as if I were a fool. But
those who sin____ and yet seem were to pre - vail. But

fee - ble is their re - proof, and
saints, fight the their faith - ful____ fight!

firm is the fi - nal____ truth that
Soon wrong will be made____ right, and ev - 'ry

288

290

Standing in the Gap for You

Words and Music by
BABBIE MASON

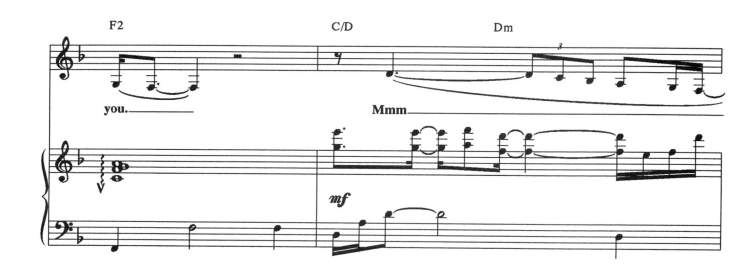

Neither Will I

Words and Music by
TWILA PARIS

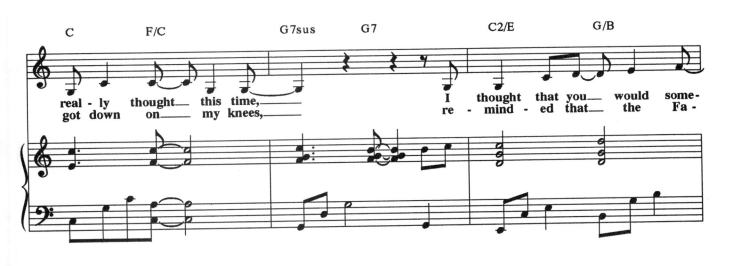

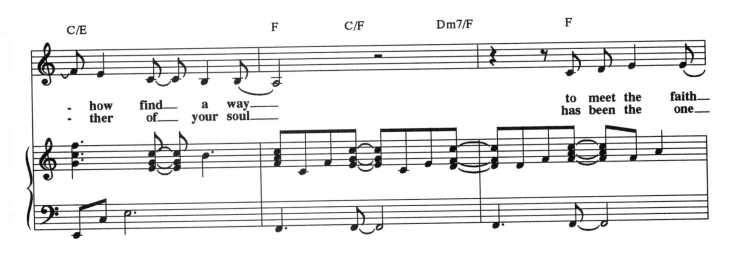

Midnight Cry

**Words and Music by
CHUCK DAY
and GREG DAY**

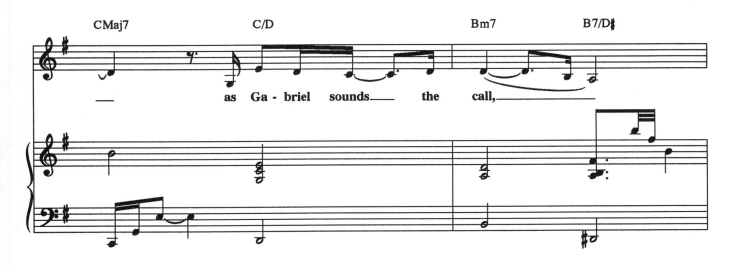

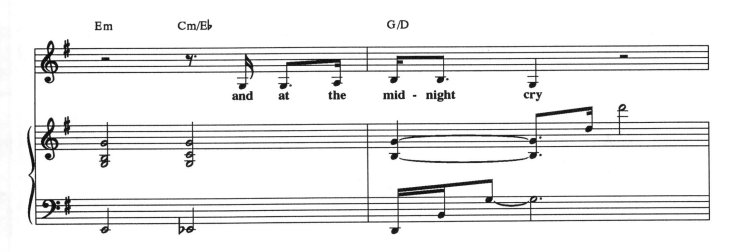

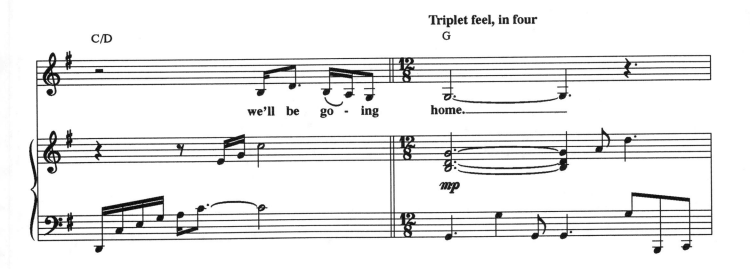

312

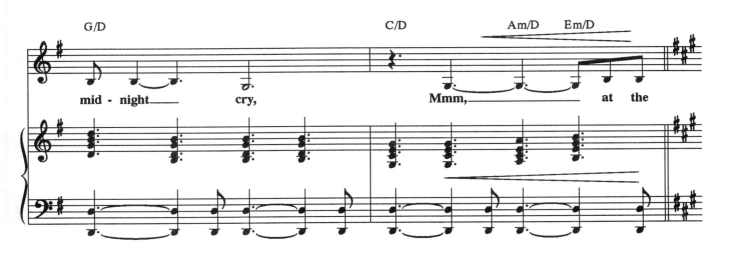

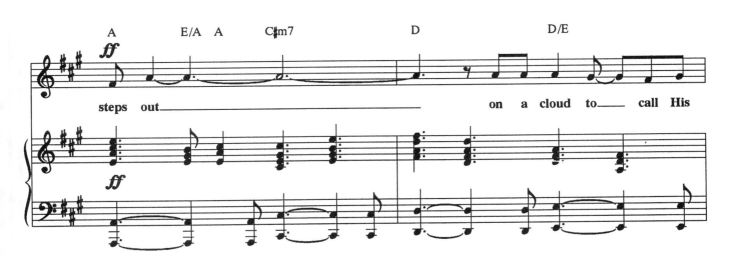

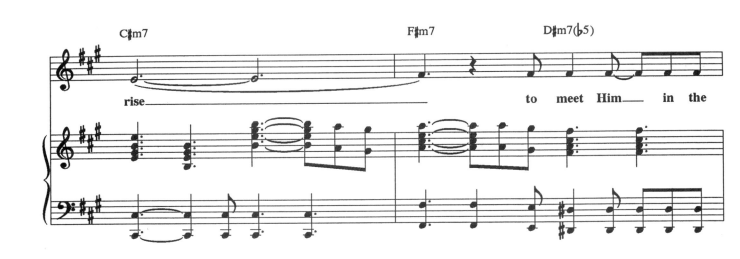

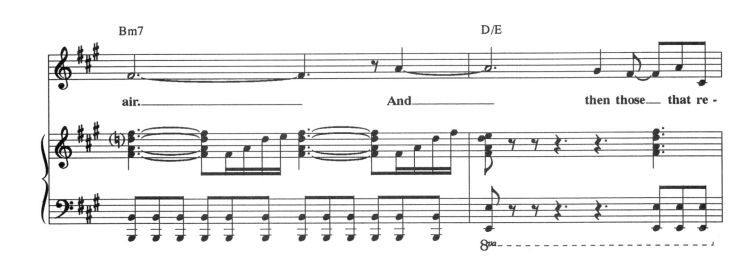

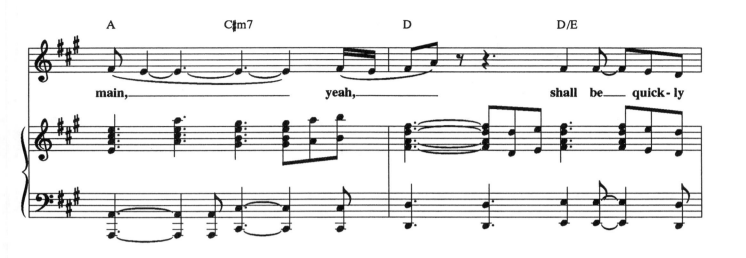

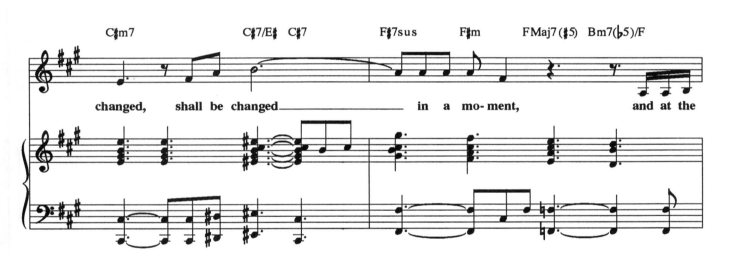

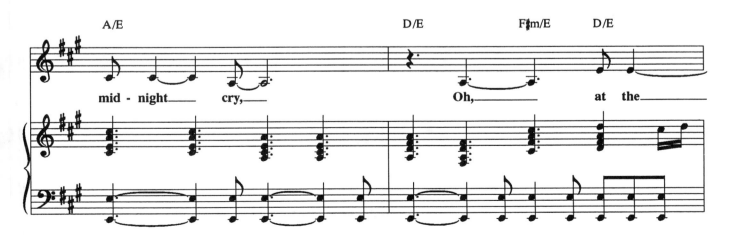

My Life Is in Your Hands

KATHY TROCCOLI

**KATHY TROCCOLI
and BILL MONTVILO**

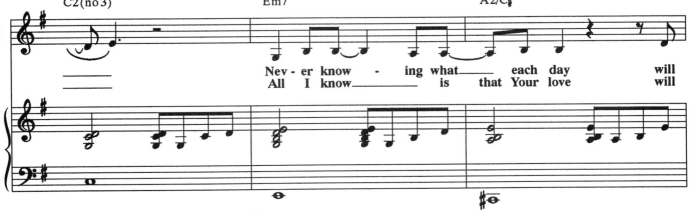

318

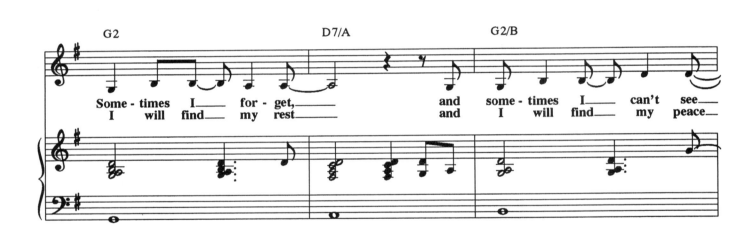

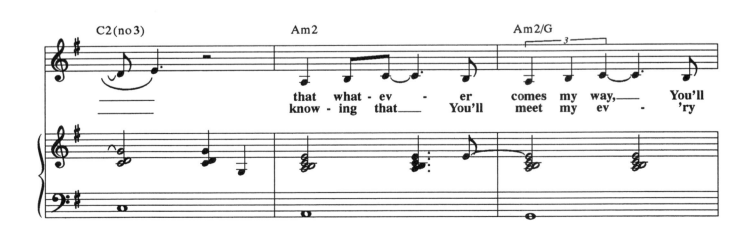

Sometimes Miracles Hide

Words and Music by
BRUCE CARROLL
and **C. AARON WILBURN**

With much emotion ♩ = 66

1. They were so ex-cit-ed___ it was
(2.) call came un-ex-pec-ted;___ the

I Surrender All

Words and Music by
DAVID MOFFITT
and REGIE HAMM

With feeling ♩ = 66

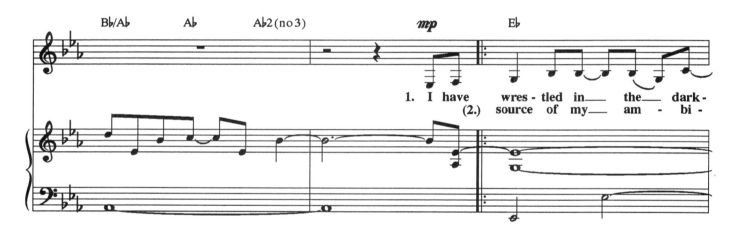

1. I have wres - tled in the dark -
(2.) source of my am - bi -

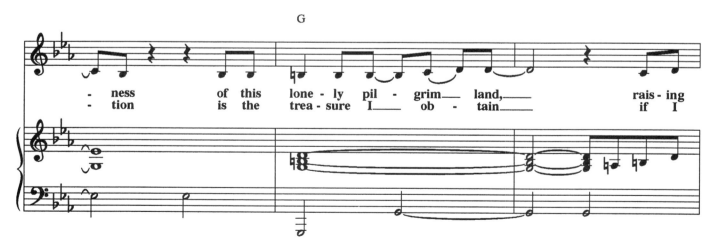

- ness of this lone - ly pil - grim land, rais - ing
- tion is the trea - sure I ob - tain if I

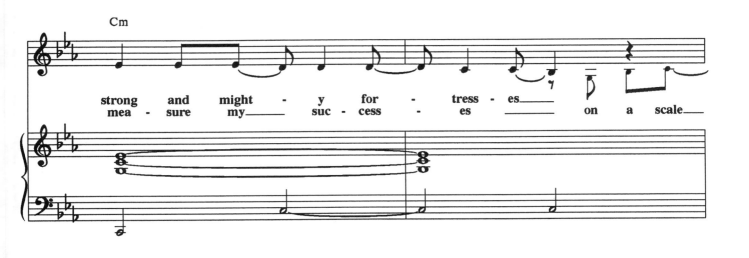

strong and might - y for - tress - es____
mea - sure my___ suc - cess - es ____ on a scale___

that I a - lone com - mand._____ But these
of earth - ly gain._____ If the

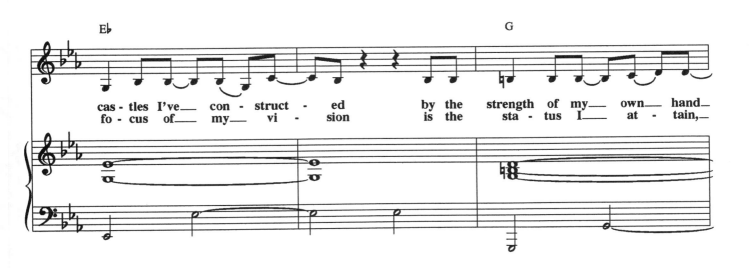

cas - tles I've___ con - struct - ed by the strength of my___ own___ hand___
fo - cus of___ my___ vi - sion is the sta - tus I___ at - tain,

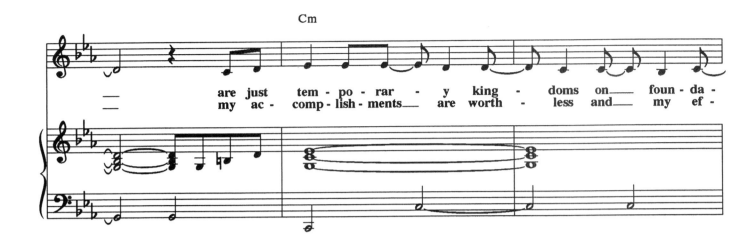

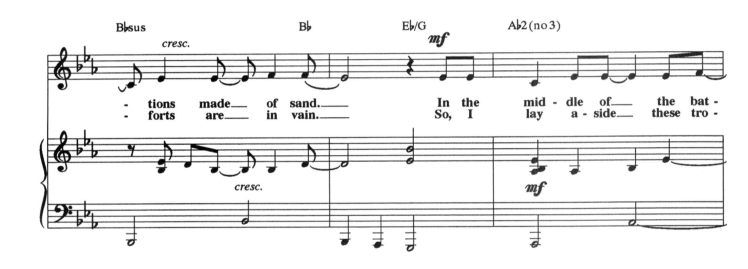

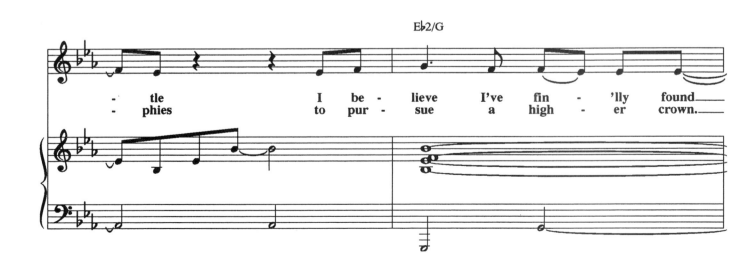

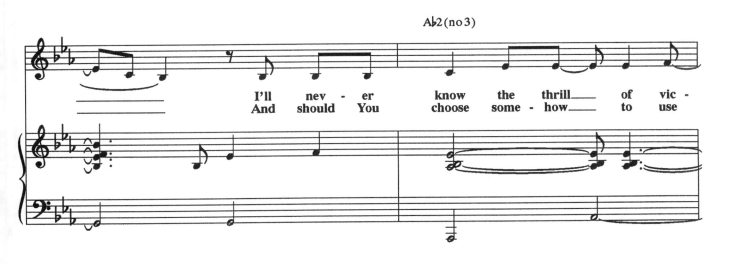

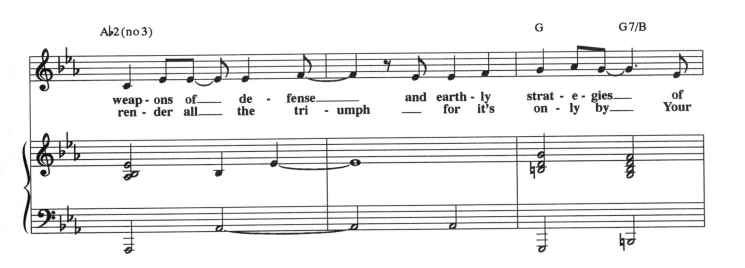

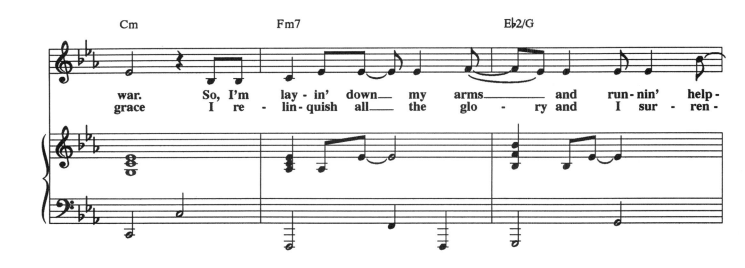

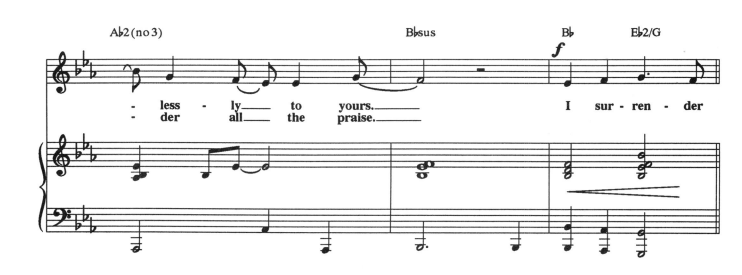

Choose You Again

Words and Music by
JANET PASCHAL
and CHERYL ROGERS

1. Some-times it seems like ag - es, some-times yes - ter-day,— when I
2. I hes - i - tate to say— that I have made a sac - ri - fice,— when some who've

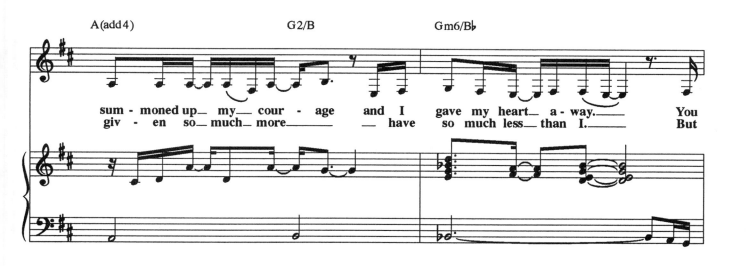

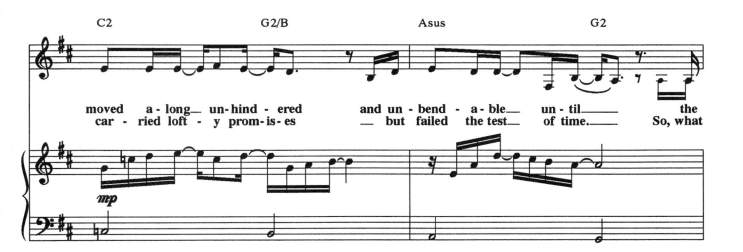

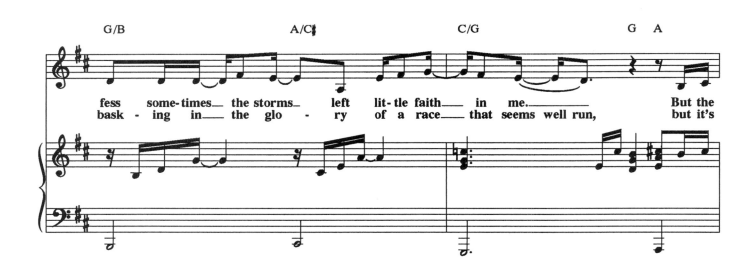

and wish___ there was more_____ for me to of -

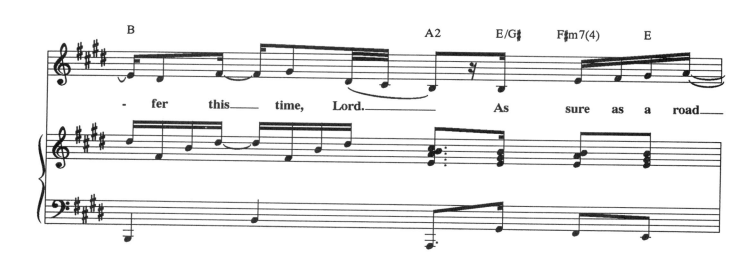

- fer this___ time, Lord._____ As sure as a road___

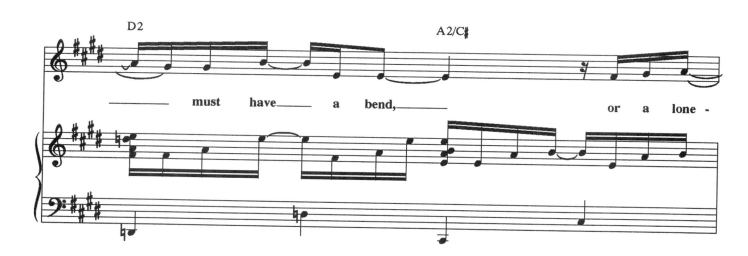

___ must have___ a bend,_____ or a lone -

Where the Nails Were

Words and Music by
GARY DRISKELL
and MARTY HENNIS

1. "Fa - ther, for - give___ them," I heard You faint - ly say.

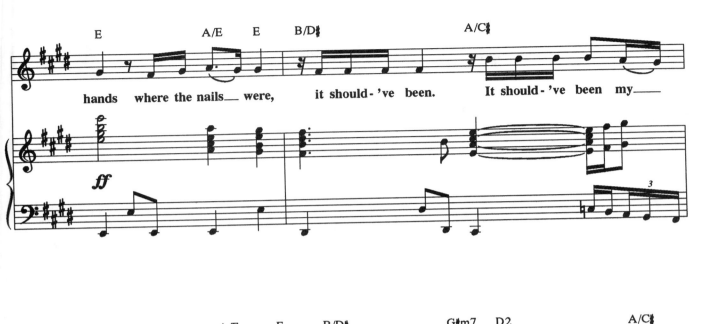

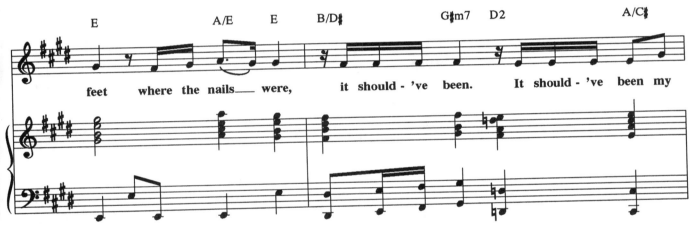

But it was Your hands, yes, it was Your___

___ feet,___ it was Your bless-ed hands, it was Your pre-cious

feet;___ it should-'ve been my___

That's What a Brother Is For

Words and Music by
MICHAEL JAMES MURPHY
and BOBBY PRICE

1. Life is a strug - gle when you try to stand your ground.
2. Some - times life takes us through things that we nev - er have known.

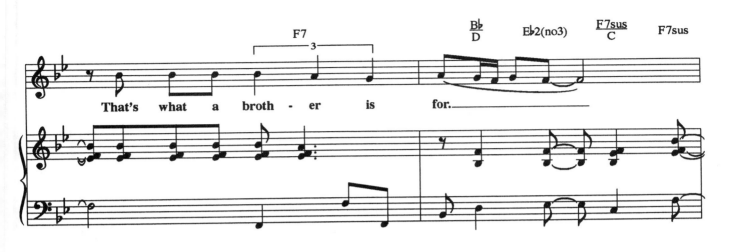

That's what a broth - er is for._____

That's what a broth-er is for.___

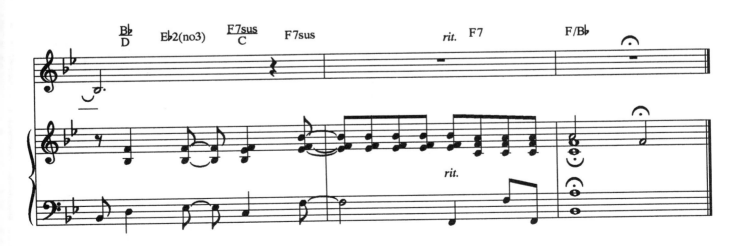

Breath of Heaven (Mary's Song)

Words and Music by
CHRIS EATON
and AMY GRANT

Slowly, with reflection

380

Jesus Will Still Be There

ROBERT STERLING

JOHN MANDEVILLE

Hand on My Shoulder

Words and Music by
BOB FARRELL
and GREG NELSON

With assurance ♩ = 60

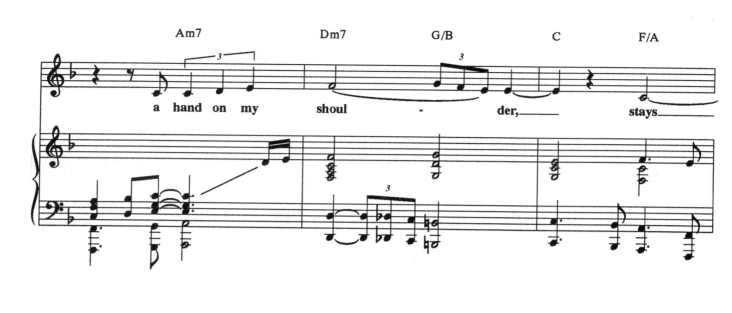

a hand on my shoul - der,____ stays____

____ with me____ wher - ev - er I____ go.

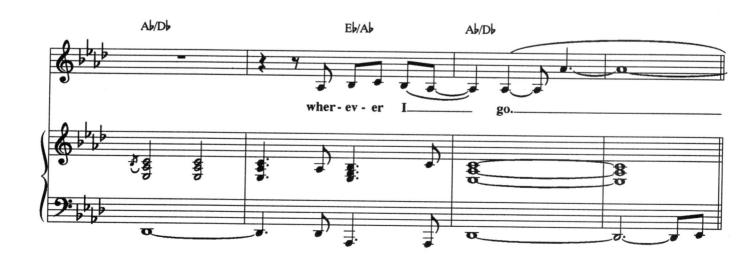

In Christ Alone

Words and Music by
SHAWN CRAIG
and DON KOCH

With sincerity ♩ = 70-75

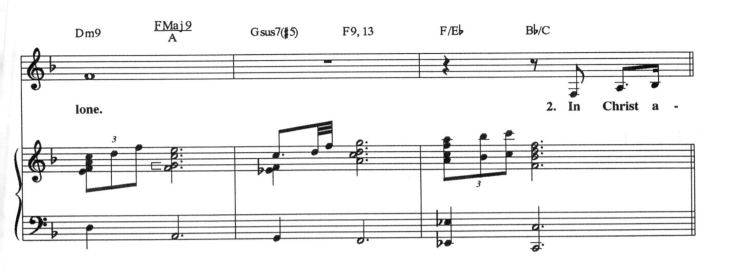

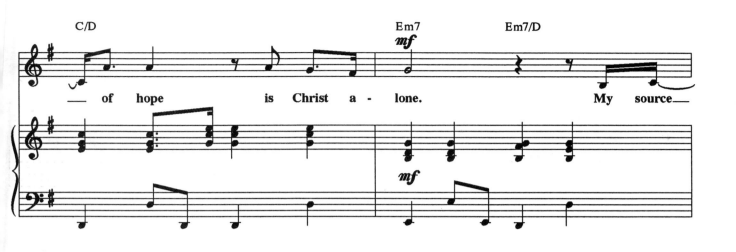

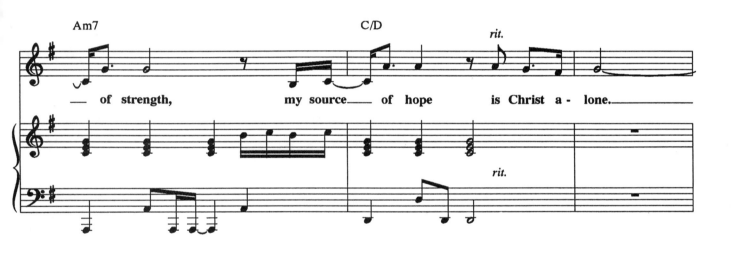

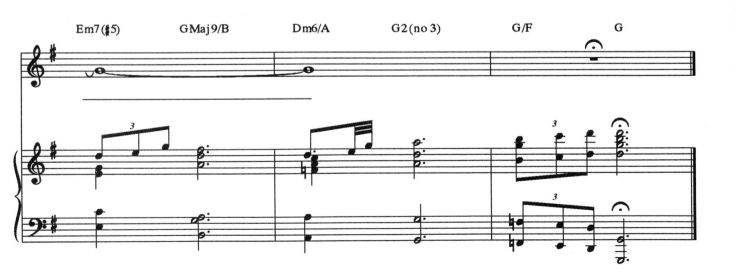